Original title:
Dreams and Feelings

Copyright © 2024 Creative Arts Management OÜ
All rights reserved.

Author: Fiona Harrington
ISBN HARDBACK: 978-9916-88-978-7
ISBN PAPERBACK: 978-9916-88-979-4

The Beacon of Hope

In the darkest night, it shines bright,
A flicker of warmth, a guiding light.
Through stormy seas and skies of gray,
It whispers softly, leading the way.

When shadows fall and dreams feel lost,
It stands unwavering, no matter the cost.
With every heartbeat, its glow grows near,
A promise of solace, a balm for fear.

Across the distance, it calls our name,
Uniting hearts with a burning flame.
In times of trial, it teaches to cope,
A steadfast symbol, our beacon of hope.

So let it guide you, through thick and thin,
A light in the tunnel, where new worlds begin.
For in this journey, we're never alone,
With the beacon of hope, we find our way home.

Kaleidoscope of the Night

Stars twinkle like scattered dreams,
Whispers of the moonlight gleam.
Colors dance in shadows bold,
Night reveals the stories told.

Constellations weave their lore,
Mysteries behind every door.
The sky unfolds a painted scheme,
A tapestry of endless dream.

Enigmas of the Heart

Beats that echo, soft yet deep,
Secrets that the soul must keep.
A glance can spark a flame so bright,
Love's puzzles hide in plain sight.

Each sigh carries whispered lore,
Tangled feelings we can't ignore.
An uncharted path we stray,
In this labyrinth we lose our way.

Beneath the Surface of Silence

Stillness speaks its silent song,
In quiet depths, yet we belong.
Thoughts like ripples, softly spread,
Carrying whispers, gently said.

In the hush, the heart can find,
Clarity that clears the mind.
Beneath the calm, a world resides,
Where every shadow gently hides.

An Archive of Imagination

Pages filled with thoughts unbound,
Wonders waiting to be found.
Dreams take flight on wings of light,
In this realm, all feels just right.

Stories live within the ink,
In every word, we pause and think.
An endless voyage through each line,
Where boundless visions intertwine.

The Secret Garden of Soft Echoes

In a garden where whispers play,
Soft echoes weave through the day.
Petals dance in the gentle breeze,
Secrets bloom beneath the trees.

Sunlight filters through leafy lace,
Each shadow holds a hidden space.
A symphony of colors bright,
In the hush of the fading light.

Rosy dreams and lavender sighs,
Fluttering softly like butterflies.
Every moment, a treasure found,
In this haven, love is unbound.

Raindrops on the Window of Desire

Raindrops tap on the glass so light,
Each one speaks of longing and night.
Whispers held in a fragile frame,
A dance of shadows, a flicker of flame.

The world outside blurs into a haze,
Captured in the soft, silver gaze.
Hearts ignite with a curious fire,
In the downpour lies our desire.

Pattering beats of a heart's refrain,
Calling forth memories wrapped in rain.
With every droplet, a story unfolds,
In the silence, our passion holds.

Beneath the Veil of Enchantment

Under twinkling stars, dreams take flight,
Veils of magic cloak the night.
Whispers of ancient tales resound,
In the stillness, wonder is found.

Moonbeams weave through the trees with grace,
Illuminating a secret space.
Where fairies laugh and shadows dance,
Time stands still in a fleeting glance.

Every breath draws the enchantment near,
Magic lingers, drawing us here.
Together, we wade through silken air,
In this realm, nothing can compare.

The Intersection of Reality and Reverie

At the crossroads where dreams collide,
Reality and fantasy reside.
Paths intertwine in a mystic swirl,
Each step forward, the heart's unfurl.

Moments flicker, a fleeting glance,
In the twilight of chance and romance.
The echo of laughter, shadows blend,
In this space where truths suspend.

Time dissolves in the dusk's warm glow,
What's imagined begins to flow.
Life's tapestry unfolds in delight,
Interwoven, day merges with night.

The Garden of Hopes

In the garden where dreams bloom bright,
A tapestry woven of morning light.
Petals whisper secrets of what could be,
Each scent a promise, wild and free.

Beneath the sky, the colors cascade,
In every shadow, inspiration is laid.
Hope rises high with each gentle breeze,
Nestled in blossoms, hearts find ease.

Lullabies of the Past

Crickets sing soft in the cool night air,
Echoes of laughter float without care.
Memories cradle like stars in the dome,
Each note a reminder of love's tender home.

Wisps of nostalgia through dreams do weave,
Warming the heart in the tales they leave.
In shadows where childhood and time intertwine,
Sweet lullabies whisper, 'You'll be just fine.'

Embracing the Unfathomable

In the depths of the night, silence unfolds,
Mysteries wrapped in the stories it holds.
Stars twinkle faintly, secrets concealed,
Truths in the darkness patiently healed.

To wander the void where questions arise,
Is to dance with the shadows beneath uncertain skies.
In the embrace of the unknown we find,
Courage in chaos, heart open and kind.

Voices on the Wind

Whispers of ancients drift on the air,
Carried through valleys, a soft, ghostly prayer.
The rustle of leaves sings songs of the past,
Echoes of stories, forever to last.

Mountains respond with a harmonic sigh,
As winds weave through branches, reaching the sky.
Each gust a reminder of lives long gone,
In the chorus of nature, we're never alone.

Radiance of the Uncharted Horizon

Beneath the vast and endless sky,
A whisper calls beyond the light,
Echoes of dreams yet to soar,
Awakening hearts to endless flight.

Mountains rise with silent grace,
Guardians of secrets yet untold,
The sun spills warmth on starlit face,
A canvas of stories waiting bold.

Waves crash on the shores of fate,
Each ebb and flow a timeless rhyme,
A journey beckons, never late,
Adventure waits in pulse of time.

In shadows deep and colors bright,
The horizon calls with radiant gleam,
Beyond the dusk, toward the light,
We sail on wings of hope and dream.

The Auras of Unsung Stories

In the stillness of quiet nights,
Whispers weave through shades of gray,
Stories dance in hidden lights,
A tapestry of dreams at play.

Echoes linger in the air,
Carried forth on breath of time,
Unseen tales with words to share,
Each memory a quiet rhyme.

Voices call from depths long past,
Softly urging hearts to hear,
In shadows long, in breaths held fast,
The auras rise, drawing near.

Behind each smile, a tale resides,
In every glance, a world lives free,
The unsung stories, like the tides,
Flow onward, with infinity.

The Secret Choreography of Life

In every heartbeat, rhythms flow,
A dance unfolds beneath the skin,
With every breath, the secrets grow,
The stories written deep within.

Like leaves that twirl in autumn breeze,
Life sways to notes unseen,
Each turn a lesson, each fall a tease,
The hidden steps in spaces between.

Moments whispered in gentle sighs,
The kind that shimmer in the dark,
A ballet graced by time and skies,
Life's silent song ignites a spark.

In light and shadow, truths align,
With fervent grace, they come alive,
The secret dance, a grand design,
In every spirit, we thrive and strive.

Threads of the Infinity of Imagination

Weaving colors in a dream,
Threads cascade, entwining flight,
A tapestry of thoughts that gleam,
In the shadows, daring light.

With every stitch, a vision grows,
Unfolding realms beyond the known,
In whispers soft, where magic flows,
The fabric of worlds yet to be sewn.

Ideas bloom like flowers bright,
Petals forming in vivid hues,
Through the canvas, hearts take flight,
In the dance of thought, we choose.

Infinity stretches far and wide,
Inviting us to weave and play,
In every thread, a spark inside,
Imagination lights the way.

Stardust Reveries

In the gentle glow of night,
Dreams take flight like fireflies.
Whispers of the cosmos call,
Painting wishes in the skies.

Every twinkle, a soft sigh,
Echoes of long-lost tales.
In the vastness, hearts entwined,
Logging journeys, love prevails.

Dancing lights in velvet dark,
Guide us through the cosmic sea.
With each heartbeat, we embark,
Into realms of mystery.

We are stardust, we are dreams,
Scattered wide across this land.
In the silence, hope redeems,
Held together by fate's hand.

The Language of Stars

Stars compose a silent chant,
A melody in the night.
Fingers trace the constellations,
Mapping stories, pure delight.

Each shimmer speaks, a secret told,
In the cosmic sphere so vast.
They dance above in hues of gold,
Lessons from the future and past.

Catch the whispers, soft and clear,
Words of wisdom, bright and bold.
In their light, we lose our fear,
And embrace the dreams they hold.

Hearts align with every spark,
Boundless wisdom from afar.
In the dark, lost souls embark,
Guided by the light of stars.

Reflections in a Moonlit Pool

Beneath the silver whispering glow,
A tranquil lake holds memories still.
Ripples dance where secrets flow,
Mirroring dreams, time stands still.

Moonlight weaves a silken thread,
Connecting heartstrings to the night.
In this space, all fears have fled,
Every shadow bathed in light.

Glimmers of hope, a soft embrace,
Caught within the water's grace.
Here, we breathe, we drift, we chase,
The fleeting moments we retrace.

In the calm of night's sweet hold,
Reflections glimpse the truth we seek.
With every wave, a story told,
The strength within, the heart's mystique.

Fading Footprints in Sand

Upon the shore where tides reside,
Footprints track a journey bold.
Each step a tale, time's gentle guide,
Waves will wash away the old.

The sun dips low, a fiery kiss,
As shadows stretch and dance anew.
In this fleeting moment, bliss,
We remember what is true.

Memories linger, soft yet bright,
Like whispers on the ocean breeze.
Fading paths in the twilight,
Carry whispers of our pleas.

Still, the tide will ebb and flow,
Yet in our hearts, the echoes stand.
Though footprints fade, love will grow,
Forever etched upon the sand.

The Melody of Unspoken Longings

In shadows deep, desires grow,
Whispers soft, like rivers flow.
Heartbeats echo in the night,
Yearning souls reach for the light.

Silent dreams in starlit skies,
Hidden truths behind closed eyes.
Laughter dances, tears may fall,
Love resides, yet speaks so small.

In every sigh, a tale unfolds,
Stories woven, yet untold.
Moments cherished, time slips by,
In the silence, we learn to fly.

Beneath the moon, hope's gentle spark,
Guides us through the vast, deep dark.
Unspoken longings find their voice,
In the heart's rhythm, we rejoice.

Flickering Flames of Imagination

In the quiet of the night,
Dreams ignite with pure delight.
Flickering flames dance and sway,
Leading minds where wishes play.

Colors swirl, a vivid stream,
Reality bends within a dream.
Galaxies formed in fleeting thoughts,
Infinite journeys, battles fought.

Whispers of worlds yet to come,
A symphony played on a thumb.
Every spark a newfound tale,
Through uncharted paths, we sail.

Embers glow with silent might,
Guiding souls through dark and light.
In a heartbeat, visions bloom,
Flickering flames erase the gloom.

Threads of Slumbering Hopes

In the fabric of the night,
Hope is woven, soft and bright.
Threads connect with gentle care,
Binding dreams in whispers rare.

Sleepy minds drift far away,
Chasing light of a new day.
Slumbering wishes weave and mend,
In their depths, joys comprehend.

Each thread glimmers in the dark,
Carrying echoes, love's sweet spark.
Thoughts embrace like a warm shawl,
Wrapping all who dare to fall.

When morning breaks with golden hue,
Awake we find, our hopes renew.
Threads of dreams in daylight's scope,
Unraveling paths of vibrant hope.

Ghosts of Tomorrow's Embrace

In the twilight's fading grace,
Ghosts of tomorrows softly trace.
Echoes linger, fleeting shade,
Visions of what might be made.

Steps are taken, paths unknown,
In the silence, seeds are sown.
Futures whisper in the breeze,
Tales of what could bring us ease.

Shadows dance where hopes reside,
Embracing dreams, we cannot hide.
With each heartbeat, time departs,
Leaving footprints on our hearts.

As we walk through time's embrace,
Face the ghosts with quiet grace.
Tomorrow's promise, bright and clear,
Holds us close, forever near.

Portraits of a Hidden Universe

Stars flicker like whispers bright,
In shadows where dreams take flight.
Galaxies spin in silent grace,
Each a story, each a place.

In the night, secrets unfold,
Wonders of the brave and bold.
Nebulas bloom in vibrant hues,
Painting truths that we might choose.

Time is but a cosmic thread,
Woven through all we've said.
In the vastness, our spirits soar,
Touching what we can't ignore.

Every heartbeat sings its song,
In this universe where we belong.
Portraits drawn with stardust's hand,
In the silence, understand.

Spirals of Inward Journeys

Deep within the mind's eye,
Whispers of the soul sigh.
Spirals twist, and paths converge,
In the depths where thoughts emerge.

Treading softly on the ground,
Where the hidden truths abound.
Layers peel away with grace,
Revealing worlds we dare embrace.

Each turn a chance to reflect,
Inward journeys we select.
With every breath, we redefine,
The borders of this heart of mine.

In the quiet, lessons bloom,
Filling every darkened room.
Spirals lead us home again,
To the places we have been.

The Bridge Between Forever and Now

Time flows like a gentle stream,
Between the now and what we dream.
Bridges built from hearts and minds,
Connecting all that love finds.

Moments linger, then release,
In this dance, we seek our peace.
The echoes of both past and near,
Guide us through, clear and sincere.

Every heartbeat, every sigh,
Threads of time that touch the sky.
In the stillness, worlds collide,
In the bridge where hopes abide.

Forever whispers in the breeze,
Carrying wishes with such ease.
The present holds its gentle glow,
On the bridge between, we grow.

Silhouettes of Forgotten Paths

Fog drapes softly on the ground,
Where silent shadows weave around.
Silhouettes of dreams once bright,
Whisper tales in fading light.

Paths untraveled, lost to time,
In their mystery, we find rhyme.
Footsteps echo through the mist,
Memories of what was kissed.

Every corner holds a story,
Of past glories, lost in glory.
Captured glimpses, fleeting fast,
Silhouettes from journeys past.

In the quiet, we can trace,
The remnants of each held space.
Forgotten paths may not depart,
For they linger in the heart.

Rhythms of the Unseen

In shadows dance the silent beats,
Whispers of the night retreat.
Beneath the moon's soft, silver glow,
Life's hidden currents ebb and flow.

Like ripples in a tranquil lake,
Echoes of dreams softly shake.
The heart's own pulse, a sacred song,
Where all the lost and found belong.

In every breath, the world perceives,
Mysteries found in falling leaves.
A symphony of dark and light,
Awakens spirits in the night.

An Atlas of Unformed Thoughts

Maps of mind lie scattered wide,
With pathways worn and hopes that bide.
Each notion a distinct refrain,
Yearning to break from the mundane.

Pages blank with dreams unsaid,
Inkless lines yet to be led.
A canvas waits for hands to steer,
The ink of life, both bold and clear.

In scribbled notes and muted sighs,
Lies the truth behind our lies.
Exploring worlds both near and far,
An atlas drawn by each new star.

Threads of Serendipity

Woven paths that gently cross,
Fate's old game, no win, no loss.
In laughter shared, in glances brief,
We find the threads of sweet relief.

Chance encounters, sparks ignite,
In fleeting moments, pure delight.
A smile exchanged, a door ajar,
Turns strangers into hearts ajar.

The tapestry of life unfolds,
In tangled knots, the truth beholds.
We wander, lost, yet found anew,
In threads of serendipity's view.

Mirages of Longing

In deserts vast where silence breathes,
Dreams flicker like elusive leaves.
The heart, a traveler in the sand,
Seeks oases, life unplanned.

Each mirage dances just out of reach,
Promises whispered, lessons teach.
A thirst unquenched, a deepened ache,
In shadows cast, we bend and break.

Yet through the haze, a hope remains,
In every loss, the heart explains.
For every wish that slips away,
A new dawn rises, come what may.

Tides of the Heart's Illumination

Waves crash softly on the shore,
Carrying dreams forevermore.
Moonlight dances on the tide,
Illuminating love inside.

Whispers travel on the breeze,
Secrets shared among the trees.
Hearts entwined like ebbing waves,
Guided by the light it saves.

In the depths where feelings dwell,
Love's true essence weaves its spell.
Tides may rise and tides may fall,
Yet, within, we hear love's call.

As the stars begin to fade,
We find solace in the shade.
Together, side by side we'll roam,
In the light, we've found our home.

Whispers of the Night

Silence wraps the world in light,
Softly calling in the night.
Promises linger in the air,
In the shadows, hearts laid bare.

Moonbeams kiss the sleeping earth,
Filling souls with tender mirth.
Every star a secret told,
Whispers warm against the cold.

In the quiet, dreams take flight,
Guided by the velvet night.
Lovers share a gentle sigh,
Beneath the vast and painted sky.

Time stands still as minutes flow,
In this space, love starts to grow.
With each heartbeat, we unite,
Bathed in fondness of the night.

Echoes of the Heart

In a valley soft and deep,
Promises we dare to keep.
Every echo, every sound,
In our hearts, true love is found.

Whispers linger in the air,
Each one tells of love and care.
Resonating through the days,
Guiding us in countless ways.

Through the laughter and the tears,
Love's a melody that nears.
In the silence, hear the song,
An echo where we both belong.

Fading softly, yet so near,
In each heartbeat, we can hear.
Echoes of the heart remain,
In the love we've come to gain.

When Shadows Dance

As the sun sinks low and dips,
Moonlight casts its gentle scripts.
In the twilight's tender glance,
Secrets rise when shadows dance.

Figures twirl in velvet night,
Lost in dreams, a wondrous sight.
Every heartbeat feels the sway,
In this moment, we will stay.

Flickering lights, they play their part,
Guiding souls that seek to start.
In the darkness, we find light,
When shadows dance, love takes flight.

Hand in hand, we take the chance,
Spinning gently in romance.
With each step, we come alive,
In the shadows, love will thrive.

Whispers of the Unseen

In the quiet of the night,
Secrets float like gentle sighs.
Stars shimmer with a tender light,
While shadows dance in moonlit skies.

Softly, time begins to bend,
Carrying tales of yesteryears.
Every whisper finds its friend,
As silence cradles hidden fears.

Beneath the surface, dreams reside,
Echoes of what once was true.
In stillness, worlds collide,
Painting visions in hues of blue.

Each breath a story left to tell,
Of choices made and paths untread.
In this haven, all is well,
Where every thought is gently fed.

Chasing Shadows at Dusk

As daylight fades and dusk ascends,
Shadows stretch and start to merge.
Whispers of past lives in the bends,
Eager hearts begin to surge.

Moonlight spills like silver wine,
Creating paths where secrets lie.
With each step, we'll intertwine,
While watching the fading sky.

The horizon blurs, colors mix,
Dreams awaken in twilight's glow.
In this silence, fear unfix,
And love finds space to grow.

Together, we'll embrace the dark,
In shadows, truths begin to bloom.
As night reveals its hidden spark,
We'll chase the magic through the gloom.

The Language of Forgotten Wishes

Beneath the surface of our dreams,
Lies a language soft and sweet.
Whispers float on moonlit beams,
Telling tales of hearts that beat.

In every sigh, a wish resides,
Yearning for the touch of fate.
Lost within, the spirit hides,
Waiting for love to navigate.

With every star that graces night,
Hope awakens, glimmering bright.
For wishes are the silent flight,
Of hearts that yearn for shared delight.

In this quiet, we will find,
The echoes of dreams made real.
A tapestry of hearts entwined,
In the language of what we feel.

A Tapestry of Nighttime Echoes

In the embrace of velvet skies,
Night sings softly, rich and deep.
Each star is stitched with lullabies,
Woven with the dreams we keep.

Whispers travel on the breeze,
Carrying stories, old and grand.
In the shadows, souls find ease,
As time slips gently from our hands.

Moonbeams drape the world in grace,
Casting light on hidden trails.
In this dark, we find our place,
Where love and memory prevails.

A tapestry of echoes grows,
Threaded with our hopes and fears.
In the quiet, magic flows,
In the symphony of years.

The Horizon of Intuition

Upon the canvas, secrets lie,
Whispers of dreams that soar on high.
In silent depths, the truth shall wake,
To guide the heart, and choices make.

The sun dips low, the shadows play,
In twilight's glow, we find our way.
With every pulse, the answers gleam,
A gentle nudge, a guiding beam.

Through winding paths, we wander free,
The pulse of life, a melody.
Trust in the tides, the ebb and flow,
For intuition's light will always show.

As stars align in night's embrace,
We dance with fate, we join the chase.
A boundless realm where spirits soar,
The horizon whispers, "Seek for more."

A Labyrinth of Emotions

In corridors where shadows creep,
A maze of thoughts, where secrets keep.
Each twist and turn, a haunting sound,
Lost in the depths where joy is found.

Fractured mirrors, reflecting pain,
Love and sorrow, a tangled chain.
With every heartbeat, pathways shift,
Emotions merge, and spirits lift.

The wrong turns lead us all astray,
Yet hope ignites along the way.
A thread of light, a guiding hand,
Through the labyrinth, we take a stand.

In this dance of hearts entwined,
We seek the truths we've left behind.
With every tear, we learn to grow,
In the labyrinth, our souls will flow.

Spinning Tales from Starlight

Beneath a sky, the stars align,
They weave their secrets, oh so fine.
Each twinkle tells of worlds unknown,
In whispered tales, their magic's shown.

Galaxies spin in endless grace,
We trace the paths of time and space.
With every dream, new stories sprout,
From cosmic dust, what life's about.

We sail on ships of moonlit beams,
Through silken threads of starlit dreams.
In every shimmer, legends rise,
A tapestry of cosmic skies.

So gather 'round, and close your eyes,
Let starlit visions be your prize.
For in this night, the tales ignite,
Spinning wonders from the night.

Echoes in an Empty Room

Whispers linger in the air,
Memories soft, in shadows bear.
Each footfall bounces, lost and free,
In silence, echoes yearn to be.

The walls remember laughter's sound,
A dance of joy that once was found.
Now just a sigh through vacant space,
An empty room, a ghostly trace.

But even in stillness, love prevails,
In every heart, its essence trails.
For echoes speak in tones well-known,
In solitude, we're not alone.

So let the silence wrap you tight,
Find strength within, embrace the night.
In echoes, soft, we learn to bloom,
Reclaim our heart within the room.

Uncharted Territories of the Mind

In shadows deep where thoughts collide,
We wander paths with dreams as guide.
Beyond the veil, the visions play,
In whispers soft, they drift away.

Unraveled threads of reason's weave,
A tapestry we strive to leave.
Through labyrinths of hope and fear,
The echoes call, we must draw near.

With every step, the mind expands,
Exploring realms in silent lands.
A spark ignites, a guiding light,
To navigate the depths of night.

In these domains of endless thought,
The battles fought, the lessons taught.
Fear not the dark, embrace the climb,
For wisdom waits in realms sublime.

Heartbeats in Twilight

As daylight fades, the colors blend,
Soft shadows stretch, the world transcends.
In whispered breath, the stillness grows,
With every heartbeat, twilight flows.

The moon ascends, a silver thread,
It weaves a song where spirits tread.
In twilight's grasp, our secrets keep,
In gentle arms, the night is steep.

Fleeting moments, time's embrace,
In twilight's glow, we find our space.
A dance of hearts, in silence shared,
In every glance, a love declared.

As stars alight, our worries cease,
In twilight's arms, we find release.
Together bound, while shadows play,
In this stillness, we'll forever stay.

Flickers of Forgotten Memories

Like soft candlelight, they wane and sway,
Whispers of yesterday night and day.
In distant corners, shadows creep,
Flickers of dreams that once were steep.

A laugh, a face, a moment lost,
In time's embrace, we pay the cost.
Yet memories spark, like stars so bright,
Reminding us of love's sweet flight.

In the quiet hours, they softly call,
Rewind the clock, we rise, we fall.
Between the lines of expressed regret,
Lies the essence we can't forget.

As the past collides with the present now,
In every heartbeat, we make a vow.
To cherish the flickers, the love we share,
In the tapestry of moments, we lay bare.

Moments Suspended in Time

In silence held, where shadows freeze,
Moments linger, heartbeats tease.
Like grains of sand, they slip, they fall,
In this stillness, we hear the call.

With every glance, eternity shows,
In hushed breaths, our longing grows.
Captured glances, a fleeting bliss,
In suspended time, we find our kiss.

As echoes fade, the night draws near,
In memories wrapped, we hold so dear.
Time ceases breath, as we embrace,
In this fleeting world, we find our place.

Through every heartbeat, we reside,
In moments captured, hearts collide.
Together we weave what time cannot bind,
In these cherished spaces, love is kind.

Dances of the Ethereal

In twilight's gentle glow, they sway,
Whispers of the night in soft ballet.
Dreams take flight on silver wings,
Where the melody of silence sings.

Stars collide in cosmic grace,
Painting shadows on the face.
Each step echoes through the air,
A waltz of souls beyond compare.

Fleeting glimpses of the divine,
In every twist, a sacred sign.
Hearts entwined in a trance of light,
Dancing softly, lost in night.

The ethereal calls us near,
In the silence, crystal clear.
A symphony of dreams prepares,
As we join the cosmic airs.

Flickering Lanterns in the Dark

A sea of shadows, whispers bright,
Lanterns flicker, casting light.
In the distance, a soft glow,
Guiding hearts where dreams may flow.

Courage found in flame's embrace,
Shadows dance, a tender grace.
Hope ignited in every spark,
Paths illuminated, breaking dark.

Each lantern tells a story true,
Of love, of loss, of hope anew.
In the night, they gently sway,
Echoes of a brighter day.

Together we will forge the way,
Through uncertain nights, come what may.
For in the flicker, we will find,
The light of dreams we leave behind.

The Tides of Heartstrings

Waves crash softly on the shore,
Each tide a longing, wanting more.
Heartstrings pulled by moonlit charms,
A dance that warms with tender arms.

In the rhythm, ebb and flow,
Moments shared, whispers low.
Like the ocean's lullaby,
Love rekindles, never shy.

Memories drift on salty breeze,
The heart knows well just where it sees.
In every swell, a tale reborn,
Of joy and solace, hearts adorned.

As tides retreat and then return,
Life's lessons whispered in each churn.
Held by the waves, we find our place,
Bound forever in love's embrace.

Sketches of Unspoken Aspirations

On empty pages dreams are drawn,
Silent hopes, a quiet dawn.
Faint strokes of joy and pain,
In the margins, dreams remain.

With every line, a secret shared,
Each whisper speaks of hearts that dared.
Colors blend in soft confession,
A canvas rich with deep progression.

In those sketches, worlds collide,
Unseen paths where dreams abide.
With every stroke, a soul unfolds,
A tale of courage, silently told.

These visions dwell in heart's domain,
A testament to love and gain.
In every art, life's purpose shines,
Sketches of dreams, in tangled lines.

An Ocean of Thoughts

Waves crash against my mind's shore,
Each tide brings secrets, tales of yore.
In depths profound, I seek to dive,
Finding treasures that keep dreams alive.

Currents swirl, thoughts intertwine,
In the blue, my reflections shine.
Sailing on a sea of the unknown,
I gather pieces, my heart's own throne.

The horizon whispers of hope anew,
With each sunrise bright, I pursue.
An ocean vast, with realm untamed,
In search of a spark, my soul unclaimed.

Beneath the waves, I let go fears,
In currents warm, dissolving tears.
Floating free, I embrace the chaos,
An ocean of thoughts, where time is sparse.

Gentle Murmurs Under Stars

In the stillness, whispers roam,
Under the heavens, we find our home.
Stars twinkle softly, guiding the night,
In muted tones, they share their light.

The breeze carries tales from afar,
Of dreams and wishes, each tiny star.
With each breath, I feel the sway,
In gentle murmur, night turns to day.

Crickets sing a lullaby sweet,
Nature's symphony, a rhythmic beat.
Together we linger, lost in the sound,
Where peace and solace can always be found.

With every heartbeat, the cosmos flows,
In moments like these, our love surely grows.
Beneath the vast sky, we lay in trust,
Gentle murmurs igniting the dust.

Traces of Fleeting Whispers

In the twilight's glow, whispers wane,
Fleeting moments, a soft refrain.
Echoes of laughter drift on the breeze,
In the rustle of leaves, my heart finds ease.

Each secret shared, a delicate thread,
Binding our souls, where fears have fled.
Like shadows at dusk, they softly roam,
In traces of whispers, I find my home.

Butterflies dance on the cusp of night,
Carrying dreams, taking flight.
In fragile moments, we find our grace,
In whispers taken, we leave our trace.

Time flows slowly, a stream of delight,
As fleeting whispers fade out of sight.
Yet in their absence, memories bloom,
Traces of whispers, dispelling the gloom.

The Pulse of Existence

In every heartbeat, life's rhythm beats,
The pulse of existence in simple feats.
Moments collide, like stars in the night,
Creating constellations, a wondrous sight.

With each breath drawn, our spirits entwine,
In the dance of the living, our futures align.
Echoes of laughter, tears softly shed,
In the pulse of existence, we forge ahead.

Seasons pass, like leaves in the air,
We learn to embrace each joy, each care.
The fabric of life, woven in gold,
In the pulse of existence, stories unfold.

In silence and sound, we find our place,
In every embrace, in time's gentle grace.
Embracing the now, as life's essence calls,
The pulse of existence, where magic befalls.

Moonlit Reflections

In the still of night, shadows play,
Silver beams guide the wandering way.
Whispers of dreams float in the air,
Each soft glimmer, a secret to share.

Ripples dance on the surface so bright,
Capturing glimpses of pure, tranquil light.
Mirrored depths hold stories untold,
Echoes of moments, both tender and bold.

Silent Yearnings

In the hush of dusk, soft wishes arise,
Carried away on the night's gentle sighs.
Hearts in the stillness, beat slow and sweet,
Longing for love in the night's warm retreat.

Stars witness dreams as they flutter and roam,
Each twinkle a promise to guide us back home.
Feelings unspoken, yet deeply they dwell,
In the silence we share, where our secrets swell.

Canvas of the Wandering Mind

Colors collide on thoughts' vibrant stage,
Imagination dances, free from the cage.
Brushstrokes of wonder create paths anew,
Painting the skies in a brilliant hue.

Voices of muses ignite the night's spark,
As tales intertwine in the depths of the dark.
Each stroke, a journey, each hue, a belief,
Crafting the art of the heart's quiet grief.

Dances Beneath Starlit Skies

Underneath stars, where the wild winds play,
Footsteps are light in the cool, soft sway.
Echoes of laughter ignite the cool air,
Dancing with shadows that flicker with care.

Moments entwined in the fabric of night,
Magic unfolds in the soft silver light.
As whispers of dreams twirl and glide near,
Swaying together, the night hearts endear.

Heartbeats in the Twilight

As day bids farewell and stars start to gleam,
Pulse of the twilight begins to redeem.
In the soft twilight, our secrets unfurl,
Tangled together in this timeless whirl.

Each heartbeat whispers tales rich and fine,
Binding two souls in the cool night's design.
Under the heavens, where wishes ignite,
We find our promise in the arms of the night.

Threads of the Unseen

In shadows where whispers dwell,
Secrets weave their silent spell.
Gentle hands with care ignite,
Threads of fate in the night.

Each strand a story left untold,
Woven dreams, both brave and bold.
Hidden tapestries come alive,
In the dark, they softly thrive.

Time unravels, yet binds us near,
Unseen forces, crystal clear.
In the silence, we can feel,
What the heart longs to reveal.

So let us walk this quiet road,
Where every step and glance is owed.
To the threads we cannot see,
That connect you and me.

Beneath the Silken Sky

Stars sprinkle dreams on velvet night,
Softly glowing, a gentle light.
Clouds drift by, in whispers sigh,
Beneath the silken, starlit sky.

Moonlit paths begin to glow,
Casting shadows, warmth to sow.
Every heartbeat, a secret shared,
In this moment, souls are bared.

The night air dances, sweet and low,
Carrying wishes, a stirring flow.
Magic lingers, as dreams awake,
In the stillness, silence breaks.

Let us linger, here we'll stay,
Till dawn arrives to steal away.
Hand in hand, we trace the light,
Beneath the silken sky so bright.

A Tapestry of Wishes

In a world where wishes spin,
Threads of hope begin to thin.
Kites of dreams soar high above,
Weaving tales of endless love.

Every heart, a silent plea,
Crafting visions yet to see.
Colors blend, a vibrant dance,
In the fabric of chance.

With every wish that takes its flight,
Stars ignite the endless night.
Woven tightly, fate's embrace,
A tapestry of time and space.

Let us stitch our dreams together,
In this bright and fleeting weather.
For in each thread, a memory,
Shapes our shared destiny.

Notes from a Sleepwalker

In the silence of the night,
Steps are whispered, dreams take flight.
Eyes are closed, yet hearts can see,
A world that bends, both strange and free.

Through the shadows, soft and pale,
A journey made without a trail.
Every turn, a mystery,
In this trance, we find the key.

Moments drift like timeless streams,
Caught within our soulful dreams.
What is real, what is a game,
In this dance, we're never same.

So walk with me, through veils unseen,
In the stillness, we glean.
Notes of wonder left to find,
In the passages of the mind.

Musings in the Moonlight

Silver beams dance on the lake's face,
Whispers of dreams in the night's grace.
Soft shadows cradle the restless sighs,
Where echoes of starlight illuminate skies.

Gentle breezes weave through the trees,
Carrying secrets, a soft, sweet tease.
In this quietude, hearts find their rest,
Night's tender embrace feels like a jest.

Thoughts wander far on this tranquil night,
Lost in the glow of the moon's soft light.
Each moment a treasure, fleeting yet bright,
In musings that shimmer, like stars in flight.

Awake to the magic that night can bestow,
While time gently ebbs, allowing hearts to flow.
In the hush of the night, let your spirit take flight,
In musings of moonlight, find endless delight.

Nightfall Revelations

As daylight fades, the world transforms,
Mysteries hidden, the darkness warms.
Stars unveil truths, once kept apart,
Illuminating shadows within the heart.

Whispers of fate in the cool night air,
Every sigh carries the dreams we dare.
Under the cloak of a twilight sky,
Nightfall reveals what the day may deny.

Secrets emerge from the depths of time,
In the rhythm of night, a silent rhyme.
A canvas of echoes, soft and deep,
Cradling the hopes we yearn to keep.

In the stillness, where silence speaks loud,
Each revelation, a shimmering shroud.
The night weaves its magic, bold and profound,
In the quiet of darkness, new truths abound.

Cascades of Emotion

Tides of feeling surge and recede,
Cascades of passion, a heart's true need.
Flowing like rivers, they twist and turn,
In the depths of the soul, new fires burn.

Joy splashes bright, like a sunbeam's kiss,
While sorrow seeps like a hidden abyss.
Every wave carries whispers untold,
In cascades of emotion, brave and bold.

Moments suspend, clinging like dew,
Each droplet reflects a life lived true.
They swirl in currents, tempestuous, free,
A dance of the spirit, wild as the sea.

In this waterfall of feelings unleashed,
We find what we seek; our souls are a feast.
Embracing the flow that never stands still,
Cascades of emotion, a testament to will.

The Palette of Night's Embrace

In the canvas of night, colors unfold,
Brush strokes of silence, stories untold.
Shades of indigo, velvet and deep,
Painting the dreams that the midnight keeps.

Stars sprinkle glitter, a cosmic design,
Each twinkle a whisper, a tale to entwine.
With hues of the dusk, twilight ignites,
A tapestry woven with soft, shining lights.

Through the deepening blue, shadows take flight,
Framing the corners of the tranquil night.
The palette is rich with the heart's subtle grace,
In the art of existence, we find our place.

As dawn's gentle fingers begin to appear,
The colors dissolve, yet the memories stay clear.
In the palette of night, love's echoes have traced,
An embrace everlasting, forever embraced.

Navigating the Dreamscape

In whispers of the night, we glide,
Through shadows where secrets hide.
Stars above us softly gleam,
Guiding us through the dreamer's stream.

A tapestry of thoughts unfurled,
Each thread connects our drifting world.
Midst the fog, we chase the light,
Finding solace in the flight.

In quiet realms where echoes play,
We lose ourselves, then find our way.
With each step, we take the chance,
To weave our hopes in a mystic dance.

When dawn arrives to steal the night,
We clutch the dreams that feel so right.
As morning breaks, we bid adieu,
To dreamscapes where our spirits flew.

Melodies of Quiet Desires

In the stillness, whispers flow,
Soft harmonies that gently grow.
Every beat, a yearning heart,
A symphony that won't depart.

The nightingale sings sweet and low,
To hearts entangled in love's glow.
Notes that linger in the air,
Echoes of a longing rare.

In secret corners, dreams take flight,
Where wishes dance in pale moonlight.
Each chord strikes in tender ways,
A melody that forever stays.

As stars align, desires bloom,
Filling the void, dispelling gloom.
In the silence, hear the call,
Of quiet dreams that beckon all.

When Sleep Becomes a Canvas

In twilight's hush, the mind will paint,
A world where shadows softly faint.
Each stroke a dream, a crafted scene,
Where wishes linger, pure and keen.

Colors swirl in vibrant hues,
A palette filled with heartfelt views.
Imagination's brush in hand,
We sculpt our hopes on slumber's land.

As visions dance upon the sheet,
We find our hearts in every beat.
A canvas wide, a tale to weave,
In dreams where we can dare believe.

When dawn breaks forth and dreams depart,
The canvas holds our hidden heart.
In waking moments, we recall,
The dream that painted life for all.

The Echo Chamber of the Soul

In silence deep and shadows cast,
Reflections of our journeys past.
Whispers linger in hollow space,
Resonating with time's embrace.

Each thought a note, a haunting tune,
Carried forth by the silver moon.
In echoes, we find our truest self,
Lost in realms of forgotten wealth.

Riddles spoken, secrets shared,
Reverberating, hearts laid bare.
Through every sound, we come alive,
In this chamber where spirits thrive.

So listen close to what you hear,
Let echoes guide you, cast off fear.
In the depths of your gentle soul,
The whispers lead you to be whole.

Serpents of Enchantment

In the garden where whispers weave,
Serpents dance beneath the leaves.
Their scales shimmer with secret lore,
Enchanting hearts that seek for more.

Beneath the moon's soft silver glow,
They twist and turn in gentle flow.
With every move, a spell is cast,
In dreams, their magic holds us fast.

Through tangled paths, their song is clear,
Each note a promise, pure and near.
Entwined in shadows, they tempt the night,
Guiding lost souls toward the light.

Yet beware the charm they bear,
In beauty rests a hidden snare.
For once you taste their bewitching kiss,
You'll long for worlds you've come to miss.

A Journey Without Boundaries

Across the hills where echoes play,
We find our path, come what may.
With every step, the world unfolds,
A tale of dreams that never grows old.

The rivers whisper ancient truths,
In every twist, the spirit soothes.
Mountains loom like distant dreams,
Inviting us to unfurl our seams.

No fences hold the heart so free,
As we explore this vast tapestry.
Each sunrise paints a brand-new sky,
While stars remind us we can fly.

With open hearts, we seek, we find,
A journey forged in dreams entwined.
Together, hand in hand we roam,
Beyond the borders we call home.

Shadows Cast by Daylight

In the arms of dawn's first light,
Shadows dance, taking their flight.
They stretch and loom on walls so bare,
A silent story drifting through air.

Each moment holds a fleeting shade,
In bright encounters, softly laid.
The sun ignites what night concealed,
In daylight's grip, our truths revealed.

Yet in their depths, the mysteries stay,
Whispering secrets of yesterday.
In every shadow, a tale is spun,
Of battles fought, of lost and won.

At dusk, they weave a grand ballet,
As twilight beckons, they sway away.
But when the night bids light goodbye,
The shadows linger, never shy.

Between the Lines of Consciousness

In the margins where thoughts collide,
We map the feelings we can't hide.
With every brush of pen on page,
We unveil the heart that holds our rage.

Between the lines, the whispers flow,
Emotions dance, a subtle show.
In ink, our burdens find their release,
Craving moments of quiet peace.

The silence speaks in vivid hues,
Each word a thread in vibrant views.
Here, dreams awaken and collide,
As fears and hopes shift side by side.

In the tapestry of thoughts we weave,
Life's complexities we can perceive.
Between each line, existence sways,
A symphony of our silent plays.

Portraits of the Unvoiced

In shadows cling the silent cries,
Whispers caught beneath the sighs.
Eyes that gleam with untold tales,
Hearts that beat like fluttering sails.

In crowded rooms, they stand apart,
A tapestry of unshared art.
Lingering thoughts, a fragile glow,
Seen by few, the world will know.

Words unspoken, a haunting sound,
In their silence, truths abound.
Echoes chase the fleeting light,
Painting dreams in the dead of night.

Yet in silence, strength resides,
A quiet storm that never hides.
For every voice that goes unheard,
A world awaits, in every word.

Transcending the Mundane

Beneath the grind of daily life,
Dreams awaken, smooth the strife.
Wonders hide in plain sight here,
Moments whispered, crystal clear.

In morning dew on blades of grass,
The mundane glimmers, cannot pass.
A child's laughter, a dance of light,
Colors burst while shadows fight.

Daily routines, a weary chain,
Yet joy blooms with the softest rain.
Each step taken, a chance to soar,
Finding magic, evermore.

With open heart, let visions unfold,
In simplest acts, life's treasures told.
Transcend the mundane, seek the day,
Embrace the beauty, come what may.

An Odyssey of Moods

Through valleys deep and mountains high,
Emotions ebb and flow like the tide.
From joy to sorrow, each tangled thread,
A journey unfurls where hearts have led.

Sunrise brings the warmth of hope,
Under clouded skies, we learn to cope.
Each shade of feeling a vital key,
Unlocking doors to who we can be.

In laughter's light and despair's embrace,
We navigate life at a swift pace.
Euphoria dances; sadness, it creeps,
An odyssey where the heart boldly leaps.

Through storms we rise, in peace we bask,
In every moment, a powerful task.
The palette of life paints us anew,
A masterpiece crafted from every hue.

The Sanctum of Reflection

In quiet corners where shadows rest,
The mind finds solace, a welcome guest.
Within this sanctum, thoughts entwine,
Echoes linger, as stars align.

Mirrors hold the truths we seek,
In gentle whispers, the soul can speak.
With every pause, a chance to see,
The layers deep that make us free.

In stillness, wisdom starts to bloom,
Filling the air with fragrant room.
A sanctuary carved from time,
Each sigh a rhythm, each beat a rhyme.

In this haven, dreams take flight,
Guiding paths through the darkest night.
Here we gather, hearts laid bare,
In the sanctum of reflection, we find our care.

Flickers of Light in the Abyss

In the dark, a spark does gleam,
Lost in shadows, a fragile dream.
Whispers call from depths below,
Hope that flickers, soft and slow.

Torn between what was and is,
Each heartbeat sings its quiet fizz.
Stars may fade in endless night,
Yet still we search for flickers of light.

Through tangled roots and whispered breeze,
Courage blooms with fragile ease.
Even in despair's embrace,
We find the will to seek our grace.

So let the shadows softly blend,
For in the dark, light may extend.
A testament to those who fight,
Flickers of hope in the abyss's night.

Voices of the Undiscovered

In the silence, secrets sigh,
Murming tales that drift and fly.
Beneath the surface, dreams awake,
Echoes of paths we dare to take.

Whispers linger in the mist,
Calling forth what we have missed.
Forgotten songs of ancient lore,
Voices yearning to explore.

In every shadow, stories bloom,
Waiting in the quiet gloom.
Each heartbeat pulses with desire,
Voices rise like smoke from fire.

Through unmarked trails, we wander free,
Listening close, we find the key.
To worlds of wonder, unexplored,
Voices of the undiscovered soared.

The Palette of Inner Whispers

Colors blend in the quiet mind,
Shades of feeling, soft and blind.
Each stroke reveals a hidden part,
The palette speaks, igniting heart.

With every hue, emotions flow,
Whispers timid, yet they grow.
From darkest nights to sunlit days,
Our inner whispers weave their ways.

Brush of doubt, the ink of trust,
Painting dreams with vibrant thrust.
Through the chaos, beauty sings,
The palette shows us what life brings.

In the silence, creation breaks,
A canvas waits for all it takes.
To share the vision, rich and deep,
The palette of our whispers keep.

Shadows of Unbuilt Bridges

In the distance, stones align,
Huddled dreams in a frail design.
Grasping for connections lost,
Counting all the hearts it cost.

Through the chasms, echo calls,
Ghostly footsteps through the halls.
Each stone tells of paths once planned,
Bridges waiting for the hand.

Yet shadows linger, doubts arise,
A bridge unseen beneath the skies.
We stand on edges, longing still,
Hoping to unite with will.

But in the depth of empty space,
We dream of paths, we yearn for grace.
For shadows dance in the twilight,
Unbuilt bridges hint at light.

Chasing Silhouettes in Daylight

In the golden glow we run,
Casting shadows in the sun.
Footprints dance on warm, soft sand,
Dreaming wild, hand in hand.

Whispers echo, laughter flies,
Time slips past beneath the skies.
Every heartbeat feels so bright,
Chasing silhouettes in light.

Moments fleeting, yet they stay,
Sketches made of joyful play.
In this frame of endless bliss,
We find magic in a kiss.

As the evening paints the town,
Colors swirl, the sun goes down.
Yet in twilight, still we drift,
Chasing dreams, our spirits lift.

The Art of Wandering Minds

Thoughts like birds on endless flight,
Soaring high, escaping night.
Curious whispers fill the air,
Secrets shared, beyond compare.

In the fields of vibrant dreams,
Imagination bursts at seams.
Every corner tells a story,
Shadows dancing in their glory.

Moments pause, then slip away,
Time is but a gamesome play.
Wandering eyes, a joyful chase,
Finding hope in every place.

In the quiet, thoughts run free,
Exploring stillness, simply be.
Journey far, yet stay right here,
In the heart where dreams appear.

Lanterns in the Abyss

In the dark, a flicker shines,
Guiding souls across the pines.
Lanterns float like gentle moons,
Casting light on hidden tunes.

Echoes whisper through the night,
Beacons glow with soft delight.
Each step taken, shadows sway,
Bringing forth the break of day.

Hope ignites with cada spark,
Illuminating paths, though dark.
A dance of light, a secret held,
In the depth where tales are spelled.

Together, we embrace the vast,
Carrying lanterns, shadows past.
In the abyss, we find our grace,
Guided by this sacred space.

Clouds of Sensation

Drifting high on cotton dreams,
Whispers soft like river streams.
Clouds of sensation, light as air,
Floating gently without care.

Colors swirl, emotions blend,
Every moment, time we spend.
In the mist, we taste the blue,
Finding peace in realms anew.

Each heartbeat paints the sky above,
In this realm we learn to love.
Clouds envelop, gently hold,
Memories woven, stories told.

When the sun bows low, we see,
Reflection of what's yet to be.
In the clouds, our dreams take flight,
Sensation blooms in endless light.

The Colors of Longing

In twilight's embrace, shadows play,
Whispers of dreams that drift away.
Crimson hopes and azure skies,
Echoes of laughter, silent sighs.

Each hue a memory, vivid and bright,
Painting my heart with sweet delight.
Golden sunsets, a fleeting glance,
Stirring the soul into a dance.

A palette of wishes, brushed with care,
Strokes of desire linger in the air.
With every color, a tale unfolds,
Of yearning hearts and moments bold.

Yet in this longing, a bittersweet pain,
The beauty of loss like soft summer rain.
In every shade, a longing so deep,
In the colors of dreams, my heart will keep.

A Symphony of Soft Sighs

Each breath a note, a tender song,
In the quiet night, where dreams belong.
Melodies crafted from whispers of night,
A symphony woven in soft moonlight.

Close your eyes, hear the gentle call,
The hush of the night, the rise and fall.
Notes of love float, sweet and low,
In the dance of the stars, where secrets flow.

Every sigh a rhythm, a heart's refrain,
A lullaby born from joy and pain.
With each gentle murmur, a story is spun,
In this symphony, we are all one.

Let the soft sighs cradle your soul,
In the harmony of night, find your whole.
In concert with stars, in perfect guise,
We drift together, in soft sighs.

Chasing Ethereal Light

In dawn's first blush, shadows retreat,
Ethereal light kisses the street.
Golden rays reach, stretching wide,
Chasing the darkness with hopeful pride.

Through whispers of mist, it glimmers bright,
A dance of the day begins its flight.
In every corner, where dreams take flight,
The world awakens in radiant light.

We chase the beams, our spirits soar,
Into the horizon, forevermore.
Moments like fireflies, small yet divine,
Fleeting and fragile, a treasure to shine.

As dusk approaches and day retreats,
We hold the light in our hearts' seats.
Through shadows and glows, we take our flight,
Together, we chase the ethereal light.